GAME CHANGER: A Pimp's Mei

TABLE OF CONTENTS

PREFACE

There are just too many misconceptions about how to get sex from women these days, and often times whenever I go to look for good information on how to step up my game I'm always bombarded by very vague information and generalized ideas that I believe to be common sense. My goal here is to lay down a specific, cohesive, step by step guide on how to get more dates, more women, and more action. This information IS NOT for men trying to find a wife, or a girlfriend, or even a relationship, this is purely on how to get laid.

"The more women you have, the more women you will get"

Chapter 1

The Basics

The first and most important step is:

1. Your mindset. You need to have a mindset that conceptualizes the idea there are millions of beautiful single women on this planet. Think about it: 7 billion people on the Earth and you can't get ass? There are at least 2 women per man, women are not scarce nor rare. Simply put, there are so many men not getting laid we

don't need to use the statistics. On top of that you have got to understand how many women in relationships that are ready and willing to get with a man who has great game. I know this may sound strange, but Women are human beings too. So as men we must stop treating these women like they are God's gift to men because, frankly, most of them aren't. The basic premise of all things in the Universe is to oscillate in a wave and that includes the chemistry between men and women. During this current day and age we are not experiencing a holiness in relationships. From a young age people are taught to live in Disney fantasies and not given pertinent information on the reality between men and women or boys and girls. Think about this scenario:

You are a cave man and you see a group of women. There's another caveman trying to fascinate them but he's lame as fuck. So you step in carrying your fresh kill, glistening with a six pack, dick hanging out. You drop your fresh kill and you beat the other caveman's ass.

Guess who now has access to sex.

Granted the scenario is a bit extreme. However, it points out some very simple facts. Being able to provide romance, passion, intense sexuality and display the right kind of aggressiveness will give you the leg up on all those other dudes not getting any. I'm not encouraging you to view women as objects, or disrespect them, but they don't necessarily require any special treatment. The second you start giving them all of your attention is the second they become disinterested. Women will dash to receive attention from a man that they see is fit for breeding but doesn't pay any attention to them. It is an exact science. Susie falls in love with you. She's calling, texting, knocking on your door and you know what you're doing? Minding your fucking business. Why? Because the second Susie sees that you have value in yourself she's going to want to overcome that value. If you let her overcome that value she becomes unattracted simply because that is the way the female mind works. Women always want to be of value simply because they are the sex more geared toward materialism: makeup, shoes, giving birth, clothes, accessories and let us not forget about them doting over the most attractive male with the most shekkles. Read this:

"No, no man has ever gotten an erection because of a solid gold Rolex; but they have gotten an erection from the cleavage that this gold watch reveals in record time."

-Daily Elite

2. Emotions. In this game you need to be completely emotionless. Don't get caught in your feelings about any woman other than your mom, sisters or longtime friends. Too many of us meet one girl that we like because she smiled at us and laughed at our joke. Then suddenly we are moping around for weeks trying to impress her (refer to my previous example about value and attraction chasing in the above paragraph). Emotions have their place but the second you let them guide your decisions you become a woman. Be a Man. Cool, calculated decision making based on understanding the value of what is what will help you build real worth in yourself and the life you live. Do not allow your emotions to steer you in any strong direction especially if those emotions concern a woman. If you start to feel especially strong about any woman ask

yourself 1) why 2) what is she really worth 3) if I get her then what 4) what could I be doing to better myself instead.

3. Do not try to be her friend. That sounds like the opposite of what you should be doing. Allow me to let you in on a secret- one thing in common that I've had with all women I've ever had sex with: they weren't my friends. I'm certain you have seen it time and again: some pretty girl with a hopeless guy who likes her but they are great friends. I'm sure you have also read countless dating profiles from women saying: "friends first", "I'm not a booty call", "we need to know each other first". I'll let you in another little secret: that is all bullshit. Guess what, while countless guys are messaging Becky, trying to be her friend- the alpha caveman psyche is getting his dick sucked by her on the other side of that profile. Think about this: in every story of intense romance, passion and lust are they friends or are they fucking? Women want a man with the right kind of aggression, tact and cool level-headedness that says to them "Bitch I am the Man". Understand this: being cocky, stuck up and egoic are the exact opposite of being the Man. When we say "being the Man" we mean true confidence, wisdom and various facets of inner and outer strength. Those qualities can only truly be gotten, built and hewn over time.

Men, when approaching a woman let her know what your intentions are. Don't approach her trying to be her friend. You're trying to get laid, not placed in the dreaded friend zone. Remember, "Honesty is the best policy". There can be twists and turns to this approach and all others. It is important to be wise to human and especially female psychology. I will give you an example:

A few years ago my friend and I went out to the mall with the pure intention of successfully interacting with some females. We talked to a lot of them and with great ease but I want to share one specific example with you. After we had our pockets full of phone numbers we were basically scouting for the next hot piece of ass we wanted to add to the list. There she was. A pretty white girl with huge tits, great body and cute face. We walked up to her and told her exactly what was up. Not even two minutes later we had to make a decision on who was going to make out with her but I made that decision when we saw another girl, a big tit black girl (I guess we were going by tit size that day), we had hit on earlier. She was pretty pissed. So I decided I would take the hit for the team since this was my best friend and there was no end to the pussy-getting. I let him have her and I approached the second girl and listened to her nonsense to run cover for our operations. Of course she was livid that we were hitting on another girl. When I turned around to look my friend was already tongue deep in the other bitch's mouth. So I consoled the girl in front of me and told her that the other girl was a friend of my friend from long long ago and they really missed each other. I told her a lot of bullshit but she ate it up and we left without incident. Later on I asked my friend what line he used to get tongue and it was, of course, one of our usuals:

"Hey I think you are the most beautiful woman I've ever seen in my life and... listen... I know this is weird and it's strange but I may never see you again and I couldn't regret, for the rest of my life, not taking the risk of talking to you... or kissing you."

Bam.

We weren't befriending this girl. We wanted her and one of us got her. Now imagine if we walked up to this girl and tried to befriend her. In that reality there would be no tit grabbing, no ass touching and no kissing. In fact, even if we got her number after trying to befriend her she probably would not have picked up.

Now, that example is what we call "direct game" which is in direct 180 degree opposition to internet dating (which is an entirely different realm) and of course is also different from encounters you have with girls you see all the time (i.e at work, school, recurring functions, recurring events and so on). Note that in the previous lines we briefly mentioned ignoring women and the above example may seem in opposition but I guarantee you it is not. When it comes to approaching women there is advice for every situation. There are different categories, different strategies and also different environments. You've got to gain the experience to know which is which. How do you get that experience? By going out and facing your fear. Direct game works preciously because 90% of women aren't getting hit on. Guys are afraid to talk to women these days.

So the handful that do usually score. Here is the ultimate axiom of direct game- if you don't fear rejection you will get laid, over and over and over. Why? Because most men who get rejected when their game isn't strong are afraid of the next girl they want to talk to. This goes back to the confidence we spoke of earlier- the true trait of a real Alpha Male which also caveats to having your emotions in check. If you can't handle rejection you are bitch and you need to buy yourself a cute pair of panties. You think get rejected by some ditsy girl is a big reality?

There are way worse realities. The more you face women the more confidence you will build. Sooner or later it won't phase you to walk up to any woman and say whatever the fuck feels like coming out of your mouth. That is not just sense- it is mathematics. You talk to 1 girl and get rejected and stop talking to women then you get no booty. You talk to 100 girls and the odds build in your favor. Then you WILL get laid. The fact of the matter is that for every 1 bitch that won't fuck you there are 2 that will. If you talk to one pretty girl each day for a year I promise you will make bank. If you can't get laid after talking to

365 women then, my friend, you have got much bigger problems. Let all of that marinate for a second.

Remember those three things: 1) your mindset 2) your emotions 3) do not be friends.

As we already mentioned there are various environments and scenarios. Here are a few examples:

-You either work with or go to school with this woman, so you see her or have the opportunity to interact with her on a somewhat regular basis, meaning you see her at least 3 times a week for prolonged periods of time.

-House Party settings are one of the absolute best environments for grabbing women.

-Club scenes have good potential to pick up girls because both sex's inhibitions are lower, but typically the women are with cock blocking friends and their guard is up super high.

-Bars can be good places as well, any place serving alcohol is a potentially great place if you have decent game.

-In passing; this is at the gym, grocery store, out and about, when there's a small window, often times you may never see this woman again (like in our example above with the big tit white girl).

-Church (some of the freakiest hoes reside here), or some type of club where you may see her once a week or maybe 2 or 3 times a month.

So how can someone just give you a one size fits all when there are different environments in which you can meet women? First off I'd like to give you a proven theory that has helped hundreds of men overcome their fear of approaching women. Back to what I said before- the biggest fear you have in approaching women, talking to women, dating women can all be summed into one word: Rejection.

Let's get into R&R THEORY this theory simply stands for "Rejection" or "Regret". This theory will help you approach women, by forcing you to ask yourself 2 basic questions. In that very instance when you see that woman you want to approach, the first question is, "If I don't say a word to this woman, am I willing to live with the 'regret' I will feel for not approaching her?" or "I will not regret approaching her, but am I willing to be rejected?"

Those are the two simple questions you **must** ask yourself. I personally would rather be rejected than to have a regret. That is true psychological and emotional strength. I will not let fear stand in the way of what I truly desire. I will do what it takes to get it and that says a lot. Regret to me is much worse than rejection because I would always be asking myself "what if". Whereas, if I get rejected it would actually encourage me to talk to even more women. Remember that: if she doesn't want to play then she is the one missing out. That should encourage you to be great, to learn and to become a strong Man. When you can walk away and laugh on the inside knowing she's the one losing then you win. On top of that, just like I said before, there will be others. I can tell you a number of stories of bitches rejecting me and then I get with a girl who is five times hotter. That is the true reality of it. The ones rejecting you probably aren't worth a damn anyways. Just to reiterate the alpha axiom: this is a numbers game. The key to remember is that, in general, any man with any game saying just about anything, should in theory be able to land 1 out of 20 women based purely on scientific statistics. Check this out:

Theory of Probability

1) The mathematical theory of probability assumes that we have a well-defined, repeatable (in principle) experiment, which has as its outcome a set of well defined, mutually exclusive, events.

Examples:

In the experiment of flipping a coin, the mutually exclusive outcomes are the coin landing either heads up or tails up…

2) We assume that in any particular individual trial of the experiment, the outcome for that individual trial cannot be predicted or known before hand - it is controlled by chance. However, when a very large number of independent trials of the experiment are performed, one finds that each possible outcome occurs a well-defined fraction of the time. This fraction is called the probability for that particular outcome to occur…

3) The probability for a given outcome might be calculable from some underlying assumptions. Or the probability for an outcome can be determined experimentally by doing many trials.

[Pictured in the chart below we see the probability of (N) increasing {from top to bottom} in direct correlation to the number of times the scenario is repeated {from left to right}. As you can see, the more times the scenario is repeated the greater the number of times a specific outcome occurs.]

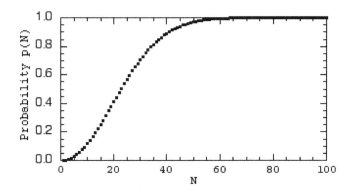

[Here's an example of how to really do the math for probability]: 4 boys and 3 girls are standing in a line. If the position of each child in line is random, what is the probability that the first 3 places in line are all girls?

We will solve this problem two ways:

i) Lets us count the number of all the possible orderings of the 7 children which are consistent with the desired outcome (i.e. 3 girls in front) and divide by the total number of all possible orderings.

The total number of orderings is: 7x6x5x4x3x2x1

as there are 7 children to pick to be 1st in line, only 6 remaining children to pick to be 2nd in line, then only 5 remaining children to pick to be 3rd in line, and so on.

The number of orderings consistent with 3 girls in front is: (3x2x1)x(4x3x2x1) as there are 3 girls to pick to be 1st in line, 2 remaining girls to pick to be 2nd in line, and the last girl must go 3rd in line; then there are 4 boys to place 4th in line, 3 remaining boys to place 5th in line, and so on.

So the probability to get all 3 girls in front is
$$\frac{(3 \times 2 \times 1) \times (4 \times 3 \times 2 \times 1)}{7 \times 6 \times 5 \times 4 \times 3 \times 2 \times 1} = \frac{1}{35}$$

ii) Alternatively, we can argue as follows. The probability that a girl is 1st in line is (3/7) since 3 of the 7 children are girls. The probability that a girl is 2nd in line, given that the 1st is a girl, is (2/6) since 2 of the remaining 6 children are girls. The probability that a girl is 3rd in line, given that the 1st and 2nd are girls, is (1/5) since now only 1 of the remaining 5 children is a girl. So the probability that the 1st, 2nd, and 3rd positions are all girls is

(3/7)x(2/6)x(1/5)=1/35

-Rochester

So there is the mathematical proof. Do not take rejection personally. Plus, every encounter you have with a woman boosts your confidence in talking to further women because you'll become acclimated to speaking with women on a somewhat regular basis.

Many men fear rejection, why else would men just gawk and stare at a woman he's potentially interested in just to allow her to walk by without saying a word? Fear. As a man, when you see a woman you'd like to approach, ask yourself this question, especially in a situation where it is highly unlikely that you'll ever see this woman again for the rest of your life: Am I willing to REGRET it if I don't say anything her, and just let her walk by, then sulk over it for a day or two imagining what could've have been, asking yourself questions in your head as to whether you two would have been compatible. OR, are you willing to <u>potentially</u> be rejected for a gamble with probability that you might be sliding your dick into the girl of your fantasies? The funny thing is that once you practice this and experience the reality of it you will be born again. Born again in what sense? Your perception and understanding will change. Women expect every man to be the same because most men are: lame, afraid, incapable.

When women talk to me sometimes they make that mistake but after getting to know me then THEY become afraid. WHY? Because pussy no longer controls me. I control it and if the pussy is not on board with what I'm talking about then I get rid of it- bottom line- plain and simple. I used to mope and gawk over women until I started practicing what I'm teaching you now. Then there were moments when I was behind a big booty bitch beating the pussy down and I was in my thoughts going "wow- that's all it really took". Many woman will put up a front as if they are divine, holy and the pussy is encrusted with diamonds. That is NEVER the case. We, as humans, are all animals and our basic psychology is very similar. I'll give you another example:

One time at a party I was in my room with a girl telling her about my ex. I explained how I used what I learned in psychology textbooks to train her mind. You might be familiar with 'Pavlov's Dog Experiment'. A famous researcher tested on dogs- he would ring a bell and then give them food. After a while all he had to do was ring the bell and the dogs would start to salivate eagerly awaiting food. So I did this to my ex. Every time I was going to give her a kiss I would say the word "Meef" (I picked it because it was unique and it wouldn't be heard everywhere). After a while I would just say the word "meef" and my ex would give me a kiss. When I told the girl in my room this her eyes lit up with fear and she panicked.

That particular experiment isn't only applicable to women. We are, in fact, all programmed to do certain things with similar 'tricks'. My point being that we are all human and easily manipulated because we are certainly not aware of so many unconscious working mechanisms that make up our psychological cognition. So, it is not only possible but very easy to learn the cognitive patterns of women in general and use them to your advantage. We will cover a great many topics in this book but if you really want to become a Master of this domain then you also need to do your own diligent research and plenty of it. One key to success is the ceaseless endeavor to inquire pure knowledge and intelligence.

This also brings me to another discussion topic: being straight forward. Often times I see too many men having crushes on women they work with or have class together with and these man makes one of two major mistakes: 1. Having a crush on women they barely know 2) Having a crush on women they may not have ever talked too.

What's really bad about this is that some guys crush on this one girl for the whole semester, or months (some even years) then at the last day of school he approaches her just to find out she isn't interested (lol That's horrible). That's what we in the business world call "a waste of time". It is unprofitable, emotionally unintelligent and mentally taxing. The worst part is that you build up an incredible fantasies whose weight will add enormously to a potential rejection. What part of that is smart? You may get lucky and she is interested, but it's the last day so her mind probably isn't on YOU. This can be incredibly harmful to your mental game. A situation like this can knock a guy out the game for a substantial amount of time. I have two personal examples of how this can go your way or definitely against you:

Example 1) High school. Big tit white girl (gosh this is becoming a theme). Nerdy but cute. I saw her everywhere. Never said a thing to her. Fantasized. Jacked my dick off profusely. Heart pounding whenever she was near. A year and some change later I write her a note and she rejects me (it wasn't a normal note I was a super freak) and she flipped. It was devastating. Although I had worse heartbreaks this one fits what I'm describing here. Waiting too long to get nothing.

Example 2) Middle school. Somewhat similar situation. Another big tit white girl (I was really into that, still kinda' am). We had gym together and I just couldn't get enough of staring at her. Fantasizing about her. One day I wrote her a note telling her how I felt and we ended up being boyfriend and girlfriend. Sure, there was a sort of payoff but the investment was too high. I want you to take this example and put this new mode I'm teaching you into the boy of these two scenarios. Now, instead of wasting time to get a) nothing or b) a short-lived relationship- he acts when he first sees her and goes to talk to her. Right then and there -BAM- he knows where he stands and receives a payout of either outcome but the investment is less. Doubly, whether he gets the girl or not he keeps it moving on to the next girl and the next girl. So now it's not about Susie or Becky- it's just an endless stream of fresh new experiences and most importantly- KNOWLEDGE. What makes a pimp or a real Alpha Male different from everyone else? Knowing.

Both of these were relatively soft examples compared to some of the more serious heartbreaks I've personally experienced. The kind of blows that come from really investing your soul into another human being who rejects you can leave your ego severely injured. Why would you put yourself in that position? Think about it: anyone who is of value is not going to devote their entire life to another human being. That is absolutely absurd. Imagine a man who gives up his car, his home, his money, his family all for one girl and she turns her back on him. He gives everything for nothing. Now imagine a Man who gives nothing and every now and then he gets pussy or, in some cases, the women are giving him their car, their money and their family. Don't Crush on any woman for weeks or months just to get rejected.

Here is a better solution to that: approach the woman as soon as possible and get to know her early on. If she isn't feeling you then turn your energy into another woman who eventually will (I'm repeating this so it will stick in your head).

Another situation is this: a man is crushing on a woman, but he approaches her as a friend! That's even worse than not talking to her at all in the first place! I'm sure some of you have been there to attest to this flavorful brand of hell. Experience is the best teacher. If you haven't been there then don't go. You need to let a woman know right from the beginning what your intentions are. You can make simple conversations like asking her "how are you doing?", "do you have any hobbies?" but enough of that amounts to a whole lot of nothing. Saying things like "Wow you look really pretty today", "That dress really makes your skin glow, it suits your complexion very well", "Where's your boyfriend?"- See how easy that is? Really simple. If she says she has a boyfriend then tell her "he must be a lucky man, if you ever need a friend to talk to then I'll be here for you"- that's the only time you should ever offer a woman you want to bang a friendship, because at the very least you let her know what your intentions are. If she doesn't have a boyfriend, ask her for her phone number right there right on the spot, let's not make a big deal out of this. You may ask what's the best way to ask for any woman's phone number? The answer is as direct as possible as in "what's your phone number woman?". Keep this game simple, and always be confident. If she says some stupid shit just say "ok" and never talk to her again. However, as I stated before each situation is different. This method works for random girls you see in public. Go out and ask for twenty phone numbers and I'm willing to bet that you will come back with a few. If you are in a situation where you see this woman regularly that approach may be too straight forward so get to know her first if you see her often (you will require a different mode of pimping for that situation).

In today's world getting a phone number from a girl is no longer a big deal but I do not want to discourage you. What I am attempting to do is to get you into a player's mindset; being a bad boy, a guy who is cunning, sharp, smooth and really doesn't care whether he gets the number or not. There are various studies concerning Alpha Males or what is often described as the Bad Boy. Here is a bit of an article that describes the phenomenon lightly:

"Bad Boys have THE reputation: hot, good looking, scruffy... but also cocky, arrogant, inconsiderate, inattentive, and almost unfeeling… and women flock to them. Bad Boys are the reasons that shows like True Blood and books/movies like Twilight have been so popular. With all the negatives about Bad Boys, what are the real motivators for women to have a one-time or recurring want/desire for a Bad Boy in their life? Are they just trying to attain the unattainable? Is it the challenge of making him fall in love—to "capture" him? And, where does this leave the Nice Guy? I asked these questions to over 500 women, a number of other relationship experts, and as many self-proclaimed Bad Boys that would participate. The results were eye-opening.
First, a clarification. There were a few respondents that wrote in about their Bad Boys… through their writing, it became clear that their version of a "Bad Boy" was actually a criminal. While I'm sure there are similarities, for the purposes of this discussion I was most interested in the Bad Boy that started smooth, cool, mysterious, and loving… but

ended up emotionally unavailable, unattainable… even stretching into emotionally abusive."

-theproblemismen

You can see here how what we've been describing is dead on with ages of research. This understanding of the Alpha Male reaches far back into history. Although, only recently has it become a concept that we are viciously aware of. Read this:

"In the 50's, Marlon Brando and James Dean brought a whole new level of being a bad boy to the big screen in movies like A Streetcar Named Desire and Rebel Without a Cause and women simply didn't know how to handle the "emotions" and "feelings" that were coming up for them as they were watching the movie. They reported feeling strong "sexual urges" and physical responses that they had never felt before! Even though Marlon Brando and James Dean are long gone, women STILL obsess and fantasize about being with them or a man just like them. Now why is this? Being a bad boy, or at least possessing powerful and attractive bad boy traits, cuts straight through all the bullshit and pushes a woman's "attraction button" so hard that she's literally at a loss for words and has a hard time controlling her emotions and feelings around you. It flips an 'attraction switch' inside of her and she has NO IDEA how to turn it off."

-majorleaguedating

Here are 37 reasons girls love Bad Boys:

1. Bad Boys Do What They Want, When They Want

2. Bad Boys Don't Pretend

3. Bad Boys Possess the Daring Confidence Women Love and Want

4. Bad Boys Have Confident Body Language

5. Bad Boys Do Everything With Purpose

"If a bad boy makes a movement or gesture, it's because he wanted to. If he says something, it's because he meant to. Bad boys think things through quickly and then execute. Nothing is by accident."

6. Bad Boys Aren't Scared

7. Bad Boys Do Everything At Their Own Pace

"If he's moving slow, then women better learn some patience."

8. Bad Boys Don't Make Attempts to "Fit In"

"Good examples of this are using the latest slang terms to sound cool and posting selfies or other dumb things on social media to get social approval from people whose opinion shouldn't matter."

9. Bad Boys Don't Flinch

10. Bad Boys Don't Need Approval

"A little self-centered is more attractive than trying to please everyone."

11. Bad Boys Make Up Their Mind

"Bad boys are pretty quick to make up their mind about what it is they want."

12. Bad Boys Don't Cry Like Little Bitches

13. Bad Boys Think For Themselves

"Quit looking around at others to see what you should be doing"

14. Bad Boys Aren't Followers

15. Bad Boys Are Brutally Honest

"A bad boy is going to say what's on his mind and tell you how it is. Nice guys sometimes feel the need to lie or be dishonest to a woman because her approval of him is more important than his [self worth]."

16. Bad Boys Make Themselves Happy First

17. Bad Boys Are Passionate

18. Bad Boys Think Highly of Themselves

19. Bad Boys Go After What They Want

20. Bad Boys Don't Get Played

"Bad boys have experience with women. They know the game. Beginners and nice guys fall in love way too fast and get their hearts stomped to pieces. But not bad boys."

21. Bad Boys Handle Their Shit

"If a bad boy has a problem, he doesn't sit around until it becomes bigger or worse. He knocks it out right then and there as all men should. For bad boys, problems and distractions need to be dealt with immediately. Women like guys who handle their problems instead of sitting on them until they become too much to handle."

23. Bad Boys Aren't Clowns

24. Bad Boys Dominate

"Ever hear of bad boys being submissive wussy boys? Me neither. That's because they're not."

25. Bad Boys Aren't Sorry

"Either she likes him or she doesn't. And if she doesn't, her loss. Being unapologetic is a powerful mindset."

26. Unphased – Bad Boys Don't Care

"Frankly, my dear, I don't give a damn"

27. Bad Boys Are Unpredictable

"When you're with a woman and she can predict what you're going to do next, she's bored and probably trying to think of ways to 'politely' let you down."

28. Bad Boys Do Their Own Thing

29. Bad Boys Don't Compare Themselves to Others

30. Bad Boys Leave Women Wanting More

"Bad boys don't milk the date until it's dry. Bad boys don't stay on the phone until she's bored. Bad boys don't give women everything they want. Bad boys don't pour their heart out... in the relationship."

31. Lawbreaker – Bad Boys Bend and Break the Rules

32. Selfish – Bad Boys Don't Live to Kiss Women's Feet

33. Nobody's Fool – Bad Boys Aren't Gullible

34. Mysterious – Bad Boys Don't Sell Themselves

"make a woman feel attraction for [you], then she won't care about anything else [you have] going on."

35. Bad Boys Don't Prioritize Women

36. Bad Boys Know How to Be Cool

37. L.I.V.I.N – Bad Boys Enjoy Their Life

-majorleaguedating

What you will find after you do your own research is that a lot of the points we're making here are universal. You will see these especially if you gather experience first-hand. The list above will come to you naturally once you've destroyed your first few obstacles and overcome your initial fear of rejection. After that it just gets easier and easier. You've got to start from the beginning. Rome wasn't built in a day. So what should you do? Go out there and get a few phone numbers. This is the easiest strategy of all the techniques covered in this book. Be casual about it, don't hesitate or stutter out of fear of rejection.

So let's review:

Question- (how do you ask for a girl's number?)

Answer- walk up to her and say "What's your phone number?"

Now you're ready to begin.

Chapter 2

Applied Game Essentials 101 (APGE 101)

Ok so let's start getting into Applied Game Essentials 101 (APGE 101)

Whenever I refer to "Live Game" or "In the Field" from here on out, that exclusively means approaching and talking to women in person face to face. The social media environment has made getting bitches easier in the sense that you can contact hundreds in one day, but trickier because it's hard to apply live game, in the sense of being intimate as in eye contact, and human touch.

Speaking of when to touch a woman. there are several different theories on when and how to touch a woman, to be honest I believe touching a woman early on is a no go, if the woman likes you enough she will touch you. Wait before you start touching a woman, because it can build up a healthy tension and as soon as you do touch her she will dive right in.

Using social media to get women is fair game, I remember when Myspace use to be my favorite way to get in contact with women but then came along Facebook, twitter, Instagram, tinder, Plenty of Fish, EHarmony, Mocospace etc. I would say a substantial amount of the women I meet I do initially meet online, many men don't like using POF or other similar websites that are free, because they feel as if somehow the odds are against them The reason why so many men fail miserably at POF or other dating sites is because you don't know what you're doing, always remember, the GAME is all about your mindset. We need to change your mindset. There are thousands and thousands of single horny women that can be ac-sex-ed while you are sitting at home jerking off, who are all single, and ready for you to sell them a dream...I call that miraculous, that's the best thing since butter on a hot biscuit.

Here's how you manipulate dating sites, I'm going to tell you a secret phrase that will instantly get you recognized and I Guarantee you will get way more results than you are getting now. Use this catch phrase "You are the prettiest woman I've seen in the last 3 minutes" I love this phrase because it can be taken in an array of different ways, some women will look at that phrase and take it to mean that they are somehow unattractive, they take that as an insult, on the other hand many will take it light hearted and will laugh....

The goal with online dating is to just simply get aa response, that's it, it's a pure numbers games. Try not to just look at a woman's profile and think to yourself how amazingly beautiful she is, because her inbox

has hundreds of messages that she has yet to read. Online dating gives women a false sense of security and half the time they look nothing like their pictures anyway, because they know how to take good photos by manipulating lights, and putting on make-up etc. Women lie to you every single day, by representing themselves as something they are not. How many things can you think of that a woman can do to alter her appearance, high heels make women appear taller then what they are, women use fake eyelashes, wigs, weave, extensions, push up bras, corsets, butt lifter, color contacts, dyeing of their hair, make up, etc. Do you know who else puts paint on their faces, where wigs, and dye their hair? CLOWNS. If you even think of the term "make-up" it makes me wonder, what are they "making up"? it's a lie an illusion is what they are making up to suck your ass in.

As a man, as a true player out to get as many women in bed as possible, you have to be a lion on the prowl, you have to look at women like pieces of meat, not concerned with how they feel, you can lie to them, make them feel as if they are the only women in the world, and make sure you treat all of them like this.

Let's look into etiquette when it comes to first dates, there are 2 topics that you should never and I mean never discuss in the first date, Religion and Politics, especially if you don't know where she stands, stray away from talking about religion and politics, unless of course you 2 are clearly of the same faith and ideas, remember you're not trying to wife her, your trying to fuck her, and you don't need to bring up any discussions that can potentially leave a bad taste in her mouth, you want your mushroom tip to get wet and like water you need to choose the path of least resistance.

The only problem that you will encounter once you become a master of the craft is that eventually after you've had your initial fun, after you landed a woman that's supposedly out of your league a couple times, once 2 or more women have performed fellatio on you, and you wildest dreams has come to fruition, you will begin to question your morals. Approaching many women and having sex with them can burn you in more than one way, there are many diseases; some which have no cures that you can contract, some women are married or in relationships and that can cause strife, and lets not even get into getting random women pregnant that you have absolutely no intentions of taking care of.

So many guys believe that being rich, or having lots of money and nice cars will attract women, and you'd be absolutely right! It does attract women, superficially. You don't want that type of woman, unless of course that's what gets your jollies off.

Either way, you will pay for sex, period. The cheapest best pussy I ever got (girl who later became my girlfriend in college) was when I took a classmate on a lunch date in between classes and we went to taco bell, I don't think I spent more than 6 bucks, but I'm not encouraging you by any means to go on a first date to taco bell, but if you are in a tight financial situation then go for it, because it's not about money it's about creating attraction. The art of attraction. Being a master at a craft. We have to look at men and women, men approaching women, men getting laid by women, as a science, and a human engineering endeavor, a petri dish that can be studied, there are no scientific, mathematical algorithm yet to be properly identified or published, about approaching women and scoring, but what we can do is set a standard, so that this will be accessible to everyone regardless of money, status, and looks

Chapter 3

The Approach

Below is an example of a step by step cohesive plan on approaching a woman at a grocery store.

1. Approaching women in passing, meaning you see a woman in a grocery store, walking pass her in the hall way, etc., any instance in which you see her for a very short amount of time, and you need to make an impression. Be yourself, don't try and act or be anyone different then who you are. They key to approaching women in passing is to make it fun, quick, simple and straight to the point, in these instances obtaining her number is the most important key. I personally like to start conversations by asking a question. I do this just to break the ice and to see how comfortable the woman is, I can be in a grocery aisle and ask. Have you tried this item before? How do I cut this bell pepper? Any question, most women are going to put their guard up by you simply asking them a question.

2. If she smiles, and is very nice about the question when she answers then you can proceed with game, if she looks at you

crazy or answers very shortly just continue to move on, just be she may answer shortly or maybe not even at all that doesn't mean she doesn't like you, she could be in a rush, may stressed about the kids, or maybe even her bf or husband.

3. So once she answers the question, go in for the kill by asking her this very simple question. "where is your boyfriend?" also pay attention to her hand, as a wedding band on her ring finger already tells you she's taken, the reason why I love to ask women this question is because it answers 1 question up front in an inadvertent way, by assuming she already has a man, she is forced to actually think for a moment "where is my bf", but really I don't care where he is, I'm just asking to see if you have one. This questions are so much better than just blandly asking Do you have a bf? Also, it gives the woman the opportunity to lie to you if she is in fact single but not interested, because it's easier to say oh he's at work, than to say I don't have one, no woman wants to say I don't have one, but buy asking her where he is she'll more comfortable tell you

4. Once you establish that she does not have a partner, then you swoop in with the next simple question. "what's your phone number" now I just gave you a very simple, step by step, straightforward guide to approaching women, and sealing the deal. Most men make this much more complicated then what it is, it's actually very easy, and the more you do it, the better at it you get, I mean to get warmed up, how about you start this approach on women you have absolutely no interest in at all, just to get accustomed to talking to women you've never met before, if you do that make sure to only get her number, and don't give her yours, because you don't have any intentions on calling her anyway.

Pay very close attention to this approach because it is simply the foundation of all the game you will ever play, this is the root, this is what all other game stands on, it is very simple, to the point and highly effective, it also doesn't require much time and can be repeated numerous times throughout the day, as mentioned previously this approach is more specifically catered to a woman who is by herself, and "in Passing" this theory is the standard, of all game this is the key for live game.

So the next form of approaching women takes more time and is more subtle, these are the women that you see on occasion, these are the women you may see every Sunday in church, or you may have a class with her twice a week, these women have reoccurrences in your life no more than 3 times a week for a relatively short amount of time in each setting, these can work well if played correctly, these women we

put on the back burner, because when we see these women they are probably occupied, if they are in class they are listening to the instructor, if they are in church ;they are paying attention to the pastor, so although you may see them no more than 3 times per week it may be difficult to actually approach her.

Going back to the standard, we can approach these women with a question, about anything, something simple, I really like the class room setting because it so easy to ask girl for notes, or crack jokes about the professor, and whenever students break into groups just make sure you're in the group she's in. now there is a lot at play when we approach women that we see on a somewhat regular basis, we can't just game them, fuck them and leave them...well because we see them 3 times per week, so in this case you have to be careful because emotional scarring a women in this environment can have adverse effects on your peers, and on your reputation especially if she the one to stir up drama. So usually I am very careful when it comes to these types, because remember, this isn't advice on how to get a girlfriend or how to get a wife this is information on how to get laid. Business is before pleasure, and I really don't think they ought to mix, because if gone awry this can most certainly damage you,

The next environment that we have is, the situation in which you see this woman on a regular basis more than 3 times a week for prolonged periods where interactions can be easily made, this can also include school, but mainly this is more of a working environment, business before pleasure, even here. I tend to stay away from banging any women I work with, unless she's way on the other side in a different department, this can cause major strife in your dating life, don't fuck the women you work with. I would advise to not even flirt with the women you work with, don't catch a sexual harassment charge, women can be conniving, manipulative, and many hold grudges for really long periods of time, so my advice; don't sex women you work with period.

So the women we prefer to bang are ones we see in passing, and the ones we see less than 3 times per week, for relatively short periods of time where the attention isn't on you to, but some type of lecture of some type. Remember we are talking about live game, person to person interaction which requires more skill but nets better results and faster results.

Included in this are women who are online, the power of the internet is absolutely great, although I highly recommend live game because it tends to mold you into a game master faster. There is no need to feel bad about reading this, applying it, and getting laid because women have game too. Please never be disenfranchised. Women love to play games, and here I will tell you a secret, that no women will ever tell you or admit too. ALL women, ALL women tall, short, fat, ugly, hot etc. ALL women have at Least 2 men at any given time that are persistently chasing her to some degree and that she entertains. In the event she gets bored or breaks up with a boyfriend, all women have boy toys, and what do you do with toys? You play with them. So whenever approaching women no matter how sweet and innocent she may seem, she has at least 2 boy toys and that's being conservative, 2 tongue hanging out desperate thirsty lames that she walks on a leash. So you definitely don't want to be one of those. Some boy toys are mistaken and somehow think they are players, if you haven't, or aren't, or soon to be having sex with her, you're her boy toy or even worse her friend, don't get friend zoned

Also allow me to let you in on another secret; some studies show, that women actually cheat 2-3 times more than men, I believe the number is higher. I'm surprised some studies even prove that, considering how much women lie about their sexual escapades. ALL WOMEN CHEAT. PERIOD. We have been bought up to believe that men are horny dogs with our tongues hanging out thinking about sex every 13 seconds, and that we will bang anything, that's a bold face lie. The fact of the matter is, the truth is, women are hornier and ready for sex more than men are, hard to believe?

Chapter 4

The Dreaded Friend Zone

Being a girl's friend is the equivalent to being her brother, which means no romantic interest and no sex period. There is nothing wrong with being a woman's friend as she can teach you a lot about other woman, in the sense that she is a woman. By spending time and hanging out with her you will most certainly get a glimpse into how women think, how they maneuver and if you're lucky enough to become her really close friend that she trusts and invites over, you can really learn a lot about women. The mask will be off the façade us humans wear on a daily basis, you'll see her dirty room full of clothes all over the place, you'll see all the cosmetic materials she uses on a day to day basis to make herself look pretty, you will hear her and her other girlfriends talk about the guys they like, you will see her do things and take actions which make no sense for the men she is strongly attached or infatuated with. With all of this comes one thing that many men have a hard time with, especially if she's very attractive, falling for her. In her mind you are strictly plutonic and she has never thought of you being anything else, if she did you would have already been intimate especially since you two are so close already. Let's face it, she fucks guys

she barely knows, yet you two know almost everything about each other, hang out together, maybe even sleep over on occasion.

If this is the case and you are attracted to her. You must relieve yourself of this situation immediately. This is one of the most damaging things you can do to yourself mentally, emotionally, spiritually and physically. If your feelings toward her are mutual in the sense that you are currently dating other girls or even have a girlfriend, go for it, but more times than not, as I strongly believe, "the more women you have, the more women you will get" she will actually become jealous and will do anything to mess up your relationship with other women. Too often many of us men feel as if being really nice, and sensitive, and caring, is what women want, yes many women want that, the good ones, the ones who want to get married, but that's not why you are reading this book, and that's not why I wrote it, I wrote it so that You my man can be a lion in the dating game.

As a strategy, becoming a woman's friend or close confidant is a very poor strategy when it comes to trying to get intimate with a woman. I've had many women put it to me candidly that they see that as being boring. Remember all women, every single one of them regardless of age, looks, economic standing, etc. all have at least two men, at any given time that they have on speed dial to either pleasure them physically or take them on a date, you need to always understand this. As this will help your mindset this will allow you to play this game with your eyes wide open. Knowing this allows you to mold your mind into a man with a plan, a man who isn't easily swayed and bamboozled into tricks that women play. Women don't have sex with their friends, period. Even very promiscuous women, Sluts, Hoes, prostitutes even they don't fuck their guy friends, so what makes you think an average woman will? If you are currently already in one or more of these relationships and you have romantic feelings for this woman, you need to call them today and text them right now how you feel, I know you may be nervous or scared, and I encourage you to conjure up the courage to let her know that you want to be romantic with her and that you like her. I already know what the outcome is going to be, so let's not stall this thing any longer, once you text her or call her and tell her, she is going to pause, do a sigh, and maybe even do a little fake cry and tell you that that's not how she feels. If you choose to text her she probably just won't respond and may try and avoid you.

I don't have a crystal ball and I don't know her...but I know women. Then again you may Fall into that 5% category in which she feels the same way. This book is intended not only to make you a lion, not only to build your confidence, but to encourage you to be the man you've always wanted to be when it comes to dating women. Now that you've called her or texted her, now it's time to move on. You should feel free, although her response may not have been what you wanted at least you know the deal, allow yourself to sulk, and feel sad for a couple of days, then move on. You can still be her friend but contact should be limited to once a week at most. Unless she puts you on to her friends that'll be a plus. If you are a guy and you don't have any particular women friends that you deem close enough to have been romantically attracted to, good job because you are already one step ahead of millions of men.

GAME CHANGER: A Pimp's Memoires

I learned that when dealing with women that you are attracted to, to be blunt and straightforward to the point, especially over the phone or text messages. Whatever you do never explicitly

mention sex, never talk about it, but you can be blunt about everything else as far as how you feel about her, where you would like to take her out, and even her looks. But never mention sex. Its 2017 and unless this girl was living under a rock she already knows what your intentions are, she knows you want sex, she knows you want to get your mushroom tip wet. I'd like to share an analogy with you so that it may be easier to understand how this works. You are a man, if you are fortunate enough, you are providing for yourself, or trying to, so money is important to you and everyone else because we use it as a tool for exchange. Let's say you meet a woman, and from the very begging she tells you all she wants from you is $200 period, maybe you met her on a social media site, or back page, or just in passing, either way she lets you know bluntly that the time she's sharing with you she intends to get compensated, so you already know what she wants. Money. ok so she can go about this 2 different ways, she can rush you, be impatient, have a less than good attitude and in the end although you may or may not give her the money you don't really care about the interaction and may even be upset later about it.

Now let's say Sherri gives you a foot massage, talks about your interests and your hobbies, she likes to look deep into your eyes, she flirts with you, she doesn't rush you and you seem to really enjoy her company, she makes you a sandwich, cook for you, if you 2 go out, she may initiate holding your hand or holding your arm, and once her time is spent she gives you an extra 30 minutes. At that point you would be happy to give her $200 you may even give her a tip, shit you may even actually begin to think you like this hoe, either way, you walk away pleased and will probably spend more time with her in the future at some point. So you knew she wanted money from the get go, at the back of your mind ultimately no matter how she made you "feel" you knew you were going to pay her for her time

Now use this exact example but flip it around, instead of it being a woman who wants money from you, it's a man who wants sex from a woman. Use the same strategy. If you are on a date, and you are talking about yourself mostly, or showing off and bragging, or being obnoxious she's not going to want to give you the goods, and if she does it may be because she just wanted the physical sex but don't be expecting a call back.

Now imagine you tell a woman "wow you are beautiful" , "damn you got nice ass" ..`` be funny and playful, "Damn girl you fine as hell whew, I know Imma have a good day today", let her know from the very begging you find her physically attractive, tell her ear rings makes the natural contour of her face stand out, or how her hair accentuates her symmetrical face, say anything that comes to your mind, and just say it, that'll break the ice and she will feel a lot more comfortable with you. On the date or on the phone, listen to her, ask her questions, try and really seem interested in her, be fun be playful, most of all be yourself. At some point in the first hour of meeting her, grab or slap her ass, or touch her hair, or kiss her hand. Now not only does she know what you want, which is sex, she feels good about giving it to you because of the way you made her feel.

Never lose sight of what you are trying to accomplish, you are trying to be romantically intimate with this woman as fast as possible, and with millions of other fish in the sea, you only need to

give her a little time to react and figure out what's going on. Women now in the first 5 minutes of them seeing you if they will have sex with you or not, the rest depends on how you make her "feel",if you make her feel good, just like when Sherri made you feel good, and you gave her a tip. This girl will love to give up the goods and throw in some extra. We could talk about the sex game but that'll be another book as now we are just focusing on dating, and getting a woman attracted to you.

These steps, like telling her how pretty she is and touching her, not being creepy though, is what's going to set you apart as just being a friend, when first encountering girls or women for the first time, it is a risk, but ultimately we are trying to separate which women are on the same page and which ones aren't, and it's best to find out as fast as possible. Because most women may know you like them and they have no problem stringing you along for the ride never intending to get romantic with you, and that my friend can last months or even years and no one lives forever. So remember the goal isn't to be her friend, the goal is to be her romantic interest, and if she's not down, then on to the next one. If a woman ever exclaims to you that she just wants to be friends, or that she just got out of a relationship and just needs time, or whatever other thing that comes out of her mouth and it doesn't involve being romantic with you, leave her alone, you can still be friends but if you take my advice my friend it will save you a lot of heart ache.

Another interesting phenomena that can be observed when dealing with women is that she may have lots of guy friends who are good men but only tend to have sex with guys who are nothing like her friends. That's because that guy learned how to melt her butter, knows how to toss her salad, knows what syrup she likes on her pancakes. What it really boils down to is this; girls like guys with balls, girls like guys who takes risks, and that what they like about bad boys, it's not necessarily the guy, more of the traits the guy possesses, that can often time make him seem like an asshole, or a jerk, or a bad boy. What are some traits that these men in general and typically share you ask? Maybe so that you can immitate them to get the same results.

Most don't pay women much attention, they don't try and please women or try and like what they like, they are who they are and aren't afraid of showing it, via their style or how they talk, they aren't afraid to approach women, and are usually pretty straightforward, very confident, they don't trip up or get nervous, they are bold in their actions, women feel safe around them in public they feel like they will protect them, they have their own lives apart from her and if she leaves he will continue to have his own life, and she knows he will easily find another woman. Usually already has several women in his favorite five and often time it's one of her friends.

These are just some of the traits of a typical bad boy or jerk, but if you really look at it, those are just traits any good man can have, but more times than not it's the guys who treat women poorly that have these traits Remember it's the traits the girls go for, not the abuse, and jail etc. although a lot of women do enjoy that as well, they fall in love with those traits, a man who can stand on his own 2 feet with or without her and do fine. This brings me to another point, in fact, you should live your life and have your wants, reach for your goals without thinking about a woman, no woman in this world will make you happy, only you can make yourself happy.

Chapter 5

Internet Dating

Like a breath of fresh Ass, internet dating has made the dating game increasingly easy. Never in the history of mankind, can one man make an impression on literally millions of women all around the entire earth. Never has a man had the ability to sit in his room and randomly connect with hundreds of potential dates within minutes. Unfortunately, too many men do not know how to properly utilize internet dating, and there is a very good reason as to why that is, so we can touch the surface on why many men fail at internet dating and do not get the results they desire.

First off I would like to say this, I would never tell any man to lower his standards because that's absurd, and also because I believe any man can capture any woman's heart, in that she isn't married, engaged, and that she is interested. But what I will say is that in this process if you are a beginner or an amateur, it may be easier to prowl on women who you would consider to be average or below average, and the reason why I say this is because I'd much rather you go on 2-3 dates in a week with average looking women than for you not to go on any dates in an entire month. Going on dates is just like anything else, the more you do it, the better you get at it, dating below average to average women will help you get accustomed to dating, it will help get the jitters out of you, and ultimately what you may find, is use dating strategies that are simple and economic for you and just repeat the process. I'll give you an example, when I take a woman out on a first date depending on where she lives and if I pick her up or meet her somewhere it's a good idea to already have an itinerary. For economic reasons I am a big fan of what many middle range restaurant chains offer the 2 for $20 deal in which you choose one appetizer and 2 full size entrees, I think this is very economical for the man who dates on a regular basis, do not be afraid to tell your date straight up, hey let's order from the 2 for $20 menu, and till this day I've never had a woman look at me strange, if your fun and likeable she won't care. Also I encourage you to not purchase alcohol at the restaurant, ask her if she wants a drink and she'll probably say yes, and tell her you 2 will get a bottle afterwards, this also saves you money. After dinner you can go to the spirits store and buy a small bottle, go to the park and allow you and her to drink for maybe 30 min that'll lighten her up and her inhibitions will be lowered, if you are the one

driving, remember you may not want to consume more than 2 drinks or whatever the legal limit is in your state or country so that you don't drive under the influence, but she can drink as much as she likes.

Internet dating has created a phenomenon in which women who would normally never get much attention find themselves bombarded by emails from guys who want to have sex. oops date them. That creates a false sense of self in these women, and more times than not work as an ego booster and illusion, and these women now have a plethora of horny desperate men who are begging for their attention. It is important that you understand that even a below average woman on these dating sites get at least 30 -40 message a day, and that's being conservative, the more attractive women can easily get upwards of a hundred messages a day, and by understanding this you can become better at the game, no one has the time or patience to look through one hundred individual messages on a daily basis, much less respond to all of them within weeks, as the person will find themselves mangled in hundreds of messages. By knowing this, this is another reason I suggest going for the below average or average women, who may only receive 20-30 messages because frankly sometimes its not you or the message you sent, as much as it's the fact that she just hasn't got around to reading it. You are a man you rule the internet not women, since most women don't initiate sending messages to men, that's marvelous, most women just have to pick and choose between the men who contact them, you as a man can pick and choose who you contact. Profiles are very important when it comes to internet dating, your profile should be awesome, you need to have as many pictures as possible on your profile and all of them need to show you smiling and having fun, don't post a whole lot of pictures of you and your boys, or of you with your shirt off, unless you're doing an activity that goes hand in hand without having a shirt on like fishing, surfing, camping, anything in a particular setting where its hot, not just you in a bathroom, trust me the context makes a big deal. Also do not brag about how much money you have or what kind of car you drive, if you want a woman to know these things take casual pictures of yourself next to your car or house. Your bio should be a novel, bitches love to read about a guy they are interested in, plus the more she reads about you the more attraction is possible to be done if she reads on.

When sending her a message send her more than just a hey or a hi, or some other one-word phrase, try and stay away from pick-up lines. Here's what I use when I send a message to someone online "OMG YOU ARE THE PRETTIEST WOMAN IVE SEEN IN THE LAST 3 MINUTES" that phrase alone will garnish a lot of attention, and it will also garner a lot of results, because different women take this different ways, most will laugh and find it funny and they will respond, some will take it as offensive yet will still send you a message. Online dating is simply about getting a woman to respond to you, it's about having your inbox full of women messaging you, it's not as much about what they are saying in a message as it is about them being compelled enough to stop for the few seconds review your profile and send you a message, from that point forward it game.

Sappy lines work very well over the internet say outlandish sweet things that are over the top and impossible to believe, say things all women want to here. Although this is a different strategy,

and can be mixed up and used with other strategies. "ever since I've seen your picture, and since I read your profile it changed my life, although we've never met, I'm a very spiritual person, and I can sense your aura" say thing like "this has to be impossible, I had a dream about you last night, this is so weird maybe it was meant to be" come up with anything and say it to them but only after you 2 have exchanged several messages in between you 2. In-between the sappy messages throw in somewhat blunt kind of mean things as well, "say things like give me your phone number girl", "I'll call you tomorrow if I don't forget" make this fun make it a game loosen up a bit. Make this your world, on the internet you can say and act as you please, I don't encourage lying and I don't encourage saying things that would be considered harassment, or scary, or anything threatening.

It's never been easier to get a girl's phone number these days, at one point in time getting a woman's phone number was a very big achievement, and to some point it is an achievement today but not really, it's what you do with that number that makes the difference. Here is how that works. Once upon a time I had a 5-day rule, in that once a girl gives you her number wait 5 days, but that's too long, but if a girl does give you her number regardless of settings wait at least 24 hours before you contact her 2 days is even better, but no more than 3, this gives her the impression you are busy, and quite frankly not that thirsty for her, and this is a plus, another rule. 2 texts in one day without a response is max. I call it the 3 ring approach, in any combination of calling or texting, you should not go more than 3 attempts in a 24-hour period, so if you text her, call her, and then text again with no response leave her alone, don't BE THAT GUY, who calls and texts girls all day every day, if she likes you when will call you, if she likes you she will text you, if she likes you she will respond in a timely fashion trust me. Women are glued to their phones, even at work and school they know exactly what's going on in their phones, of course there are exceptions when they just truly are busy.

Although I wasn't a huge fan of being incredibly respectful to women, it is a moral thing to do no matter how upset you are, or how angry you are, try not to disrespect women, but there are occasions when it is ok to call them bitches and hoes, but try and limit that sort of thing to rare occasions.

Many women have learned that using make up, and different angles of light, can drastically change their appearance, more women than not look much better in their pictures than they do in person just accept that as a fact. The faster you learn to accept that fact the better off you'll be. This is another thing that drives men crazy, women know men are visual creatures why do you think everywhere you go women are constantly showing off their breasts and their asses in tight pants and putting on a lot of makeup, they aren't doing it for other women. Well some are. Try not to get emotionally tangled up in what her picture looks like because when you meet her there's a high chance she's 1-2 points less attractive. Also women are only taking face shots, be very weary of that, w woman should have many different pictures of herself, and some should clearly show her body, don't message women who just have face shots, don't message women

who wear an excessive amount of makeup, don't message women who only have one picture of themselves, and I would encourage you not to message a woman who doesn't say much about herself in her profile, if she just has a few pictures and 2 words on her bio don't message her, that's a high chance of a catfish.

Chapter 6

Have Fun

Wow there is so much to say about this subject, in that in today's society it can be hard to distinguish if a man is a woman or if a woman is a man whether that be via looks or how someone chooses to act, or what they believe in. there does seem to be a gender role reversal, in that many women are taking roles and or acting in a way a strong man would appear to act, and more men are being led by women. I do understand there is lots of political and gay rights and other shit that's controversial and I would rather not delve into that, but I guess it's safe to assume that you are in fact a man wanting to better your game and chances at dating women you actually want to date.

I am ore of a traditional guy in that I believe the guy should do the oil changes on the car, cut the grass, and do work around the house as he supports his family financially, emotionally, and physically, well as the woman is more responsible for cooking, cleaning etc. but now that I started writing this I sort of feel as if I'm going into categories that are beyond this book so I will stop

Dealing with women you only want to use you, this is major, especially for African American women, and or women who are low income, or poorly educated, and are looking for handouts, dating a woman should be fun, she shouldn't be on her phone texting the whole time she's with you, and if she seems uninterested in the first 10 minutes of getting in your car, or if you aren't interested take her back from wherever you picked her up at, no need to waste your time dealing with a women for the next couple hours and spending money on her. Remember when women go on dates for the most part all they are doing is riding, eating, and no spending, you are the one doing all the work, so if you see or notice any red flags then leave her. I had a new Camaro one time and a girl got in my car and said it was dirty after I just cleaned it and it was spotless, I told her if you think this is dirty then we aren't going to get along I'm dropping you off home, where she then exclaimed that she just paid her babysitter to go on this date and that she still wanted to go, I don't remember her name or where we went, but I do remember having sex with her on several occasions at her house. As a man say what you mean and mean what you say when it

comes to women, don't be a pushover, I'm not suggesting that you be mean or disrespectful but whenever first dating a woman especially more so if you meet her online, there are so many women out here with lots of baggage and most are already in some type of relationship. So have your guard up.

HOW and where to meet women. Women are everywhere, and in abundance in most part of this planet, so the question isn't where to meet women as much as it is how to approach women in public without coming across as a stalker or creep and the best way to do that is make simple conversation, and to see if she's into the conversation and you can continue. Depending on your MOS you ay like bars, clubs, which I do not like, but if that's your cup of tea that's fine, but here I will explain briefly as to why I always strongly suggest that you as a man not entertain clubs, or bars for dating, well its ok for hook ups, and one night stands, but generally with all the alcohol and drugs consumed, and the girls who initially come to the bar or club with their walls incredibly high, if you want a quickie that's cool. Supermarkets, can be an interesting place to meet women, malls, church, outside concerts and gathering are also good.

Chapter 7

The Manipulated Man

The vast majority of this chapter is directly influenced by YouTube Channel "Feminism LOL"

Is female behavior innate or learned. Most of what women do is learned behavior, the innate part is this: a child comes out of a woman's body, everyone is aware of this, it's a manifestation of something miraculous, humans come out of female bodies it gives the women a sense of divinity, when people look around them they can see that women get a deference they run the household, they are the authority to children, that's a divine quality to have humans come out. Young girls see that woman can have control without working, boys do not have that romodel boys must work period.in the formative year's women have an option to have other people do their works for them they play out ways through the play with dolls, men do have a demand for good character with fertile imaginations, inate vs learned, Ernest Becker, if you are wrong about

One of the first things a child has to learn is how much power he has and how much exists in others and in the world. Only if he learns this can he be sure of surviving: he has to learn very minutely what powers he can count on to facilitate his life and what powers he has to fear and avoid in order to protect it, so power becomes the basic category of being for which he has, so to speak, a natural respect: if you are wrong about power, you don't get a chance to be right about anything else; and the things that happen when the organism loses its powers are a decrease of vitality and death. "Ester Vilar"

Girls see that they can get power by proxy, people spend more attention on them when they cry, option of not having to be a provider boys don't have the same option. When girls go to school around 5 and are surrounded by other girls one attractive girl can have the attention of 12 boys, many guys doing things for her, here's a cookie ill pick up your bag etc., one girl can get the

proxy power of many men. She has to compete with other girls, can I get myself that one guy? One girl draws all the attention of the guys, but if she sticks around the queen bee she may get one guy she doesn't want. But some girls will have to work, for looking for a provider but they still have it has their dream, when beauty or looks etc. fail to get attention from men, she can always fall back on her pussy, as in child bearing, and they play this game. It's a fun game for them to play, that comes at failing getting attention from her guy, even if she gets the guy, she knows her beauty will fade but by bearing children secure it an immortality project, men can access this without women. If he forces it she can abort, so it needs to be cooperation. Many people care about their seeds, women offer the opportunity to carry genes, ugly women and bitches can offer this one thing. Children are often referred to as women's children, empty vessels, like pets when they are puppy and kittens, so that you can train them the way you like, a little baby can be filled and shaped, women. Girls play with dolls, they practice manipulating dolls by saying no. boys play relationships between them where they make the doll do what she wants, as practice, boys just play Legos and army. Create empty vessels and make them do what you want them to do, playing god practices carry on later in life. Not all women are like that, all women are like this, the good ones try and stop themselves, but that's infinitesimal, women get in their head they can live by proxy power and raise gremlins, battered women chose to be at the mercy of men powerfully where they do for themselves, to get what they want they have to get a guy who can get them what they want. If my life sucks I need a man to do it for me, then bully them into getting what they want, most don't live their own lives. Domestic violence is reciprocal, the majority of the time women are the ones doing the violence, the guy they invested in the man and he doesn't do it, you become their biggest problem. Only deal with women if they want something they can go and get it their fucking selves

Exposing how women manipulate men, woman is information gathers the first thing they do is study men, its catered to each specific individual, let's look at some types of things women do sociopathic, psychopathic, feminine technique step number one. To get men close to her, soft skin, smell good, and a psychology effect, touching your face with an expression etc. Getting you in her physical presence woman are master manipulators comfortable truth about

How are men and women being different, girls play doll and house character manipulation, manufacture relationships, this practice is what shapes behavior on how to control men, boys play toys about building things, actions, not much about manipulating affairs. This is the formation of social nature of men and women, men focus on creation construction and action. Women are shape shifters, a woman's manipulation of a man is catered to that specific man, used in seduction is subtle, you can't trust women, because it's easy to pull off a lie. It takes 3 months for a person to really know who a bitch is. Women are mimics they are great imitators, ultimately the key is to mimic or. is she actively using her mind to actively engage in

conversation, or just regurgitating hat she's previously heard. Favorite topic for women is talking about being a woman, if she wants to get attention battered women.

.men are people who work and women are people who don't work, men have to work, to provide for themselves and their family, women work because of their status, she will up her income requirement for her man, they increase their disposable income, so she can spend more money on herself, women do not intend on being a provider, or career on something they must do, women don choose to be mechanics, garbage man, construction their career is more luxurious because they "choose" to work, for men it's a different scenario. So why do men play along why have women not been unmasked yet? Ernest Becker, escape from evil. Men project a goddess type manna on women, they bear children act, women are the key to. Men are willing slaves, because they are better creatures to perpetuate immortality by passing his genes, of surviving his own death that's why men are so happy to be women's slave,

I'm speaking generally there is a difference between being a female or being a woman, and we are not talking about LGBT, men must be self-reliant women end up being retarded. Abused women who are stuck in the house with no resources or education, boys just can't move in with a guy and expect to be taking care of. Women try to obtain power in convert ways, they try to rule by manipulating men by looking sweet and innocent. Women almost always have ulterior motives.

Why are women not as funny aren't funny, women slaughters and smiles are superficial, they try and stay in control of their face, humor is risky, women don't want to risk social rejection so they take fewer chances, humor is a defense mechanism, women prefer to be rescued, good humor, people don't like to be mean to women they don't mock them as often, comedy is aggressive they like to hide their aggression, women mostly hang out with each other, insincere feedback. They learn only on they learn at men's joke, you get a positive response, they don't know what's funny they just like men

Do women care what women think? Women know the difference between a real Gucci handbag as opposed to fake when a man couldn't? women put on makeup because they are competing with other women, to do better than her, not necessarily entice men. All they care about is being better, looking younger or better men don't notice. Gay men and straight women, gay men don't care about straight women because they want men. It's the women who attach themselves to the men, they care about home décor and fashion, and bullshit that normal men don't care about, a male friend who understand fashion, good fashion advice who understands other guys, and the gay men aren't competing with her, that's why women throw themselves at gay guys, if women are looking at magazines, they tear them to shreds and cut them up and discourage women all the time, omg she looks like a slut, women are in competition of each other, guys don't even know what women are talking about, all the subtle little things, we just see bizarre game, or something mysterious, a woman's demand on life will always be material not intellectual

Why do good women stay in bad relationship, 1, she is a people person she wants everyone else to be happy 2 fear of the unknown, rather have a current shitty situation than risk a relationship that may be worst 3. She loves to try and fix people, or trying to change somebody this can often take years. 4. She finds excitement in a tumultuous relationship, some get excitement for positive or negative. 5. He using leverage and may be threating the woman.

Women who want to use you, men let's not make any mistakes and assumptions that women have your best interest at heart, because in more cases than not they do not.im going to tell you the women to look out for that I wouldn't even attempt to date period. Let's go over some obvious signs. Before I make this list I must add, its ok to date sluts, hoes, bitches, and prostitutes if that's your thing, but if they have any of these attributes stay as far as possible from them

1.artificicail hair color, if a woman has a hair color that didn't come natural to any woman of any race leave her alone. Pink hair, green hair blue hair etc.

2.weave or extensions, unless it's in moderation, if a woman wears weave leave her alone

3. unless you're into tattoos, don't date women with very visible tattoos, and especially if they are distasteful, if she has tats on her boobs cleavage, or on her lower back, that's distasteful

4tongue rings, now women you date should have tongue rings

5.not being able to speak good English and use good diction and tone

Hygiene must be good

The world is ruled by dead men, because dead men left their ideas on paper.

Don't date black women! Stick to any race or ethnicity black women can easily consume you into the inner bowls of evil and confusion that you will easily lose yourself.

There are 2 distinct categories when it comes to approaching woman and here we will attempt to make this as simple as possible. We will generalize a bit because all situations are different, so the is what we will call The Basic Game plan, that beginners and professionals can ultimately pull from equally, but this is more of a beginners guide to approaching woman.

The 2 different categories with sub categories are as follows

1. You already know the woman, at least to the point where you can consider her an acquaintance, meaning that you two have talked and or hung out before in "several different occasions" for various time span. In essence you've spoke to this girl more than once or twice.

The sub category to this is a woman that you know very well, you've been friends for months or years and c communicate often with each other via phone or in person, this also includes long distance relationships.

2 the other category is that you don't know her, even if you know her friends that doesn't count I don't believe in piggy backing off her friends or family unless she initiates that type of move

You see my goal is to make approaching woman as concrete and cohesive as a machine and its parts, and the only way to do a comprehensive model that every man can follow is to use information that doesn't change, for example. These categories are simple, either you know a woman or you don't, or you may have sort of kind of talked on a quick occasion or through social media. These. the difficulty comes in trying to fashion information off of every possible situation and not telling you exactly what to do, that's what I'm here for.

So there are really only 4 basic, remember basic approaches for women, the better you get, or if you are already polished and looking to up your game all your game will stem from this info.

Being adorable, and cute, and funny are all very important things, but I can't tell you how to be funny in a book, I can't tell you how to dress, or what car to drive, because in essence you need to be yourself when using the approach techniques, so if you're funny be funny, if you're serious be serious, if your weird be weird dude. But however your personality is structured just make sure you are confident! And we will talk about how to GAIN CONFIDENCE

Chapter 8

Arm Yourself for Battle

Woman on average when it comes to dating are simply better and smarter at it, let's just take a look at the numbers, and I'm generalizing, an average mediocre man between the the years of him being 18-26 an eight year span, with him going to school, or the army, or in learning a trade, or selling dope etc., just a b student at everything, probably can honestly say within an 8 year period has had between 3-5 real girlfriends, and can probably say he managed to go on 30-50 dates in that 8 year span, each with a different woman, ok for a man that is in school, the armed services, or in trade or white collar business for one doesn't have the time to date , because he was taught that he must be the provider, so he has to do things to make that happen, so in essence he just doesn't have the time, and then add to the fact that he may have a girlfriend or wife for several years in which we say was faithful too, so that rob him the time to actual practice game or even apply it to other attractive women because he's tied down, so in a 8 year period between work, wives, kids , girlfriends and trying to stay out of jail, he may not be as equipped as he may have otherwise been. Which is not a bad thing thig, but there is a reason we call this a game, according to google the definition of the word game is "a form of play or sport, especially competitive one played according to rules and decided by skill, strength, or luck" as a man in this game as of with any you need skill, strength, knowledge of the rules, and a big one when it comes to dating is luck" so how do you get better at a skill, or stronger, you must train and practice, but just as in physical sports that doesn't mean you will win every time, the only

difference between a amateur and a professional is that a professional aces it look easy, because they invested countless hours, usually under the supervision of another former professional, they trained, and practiced and with some luck with good genes or someone they know made it to become professional. I'm saying all of this to simply say that in fact, Woman believe it or not differ in this dating game because, you are competing for them the actual woman is the prize, and I'll let you in on a secret a real secret, it's not other men that your competing against, your competing against yourself. Being able to manage situations properly, being able to accept that she's dating other men, not being jealous, not being a creeper by calling and texting her all the time, being able to suppress your emotions even if you are head over heels for her, to always maintain your own unique personality and if you have to easily separate and apart from her, because let's face it there's a reason for calling this dating as well sir.

According to Wikipedia s dating is a part of the human mating process whereby two people meet socially for companionship, beyond the level of friendship, or with the aim of each assessing the other suitability as a partner in an intimate relationship or marriage. It can be a form of courtship consisting of social activities done by the couple, while the term has several meaning it usually refers to the act of meeting and engaging in some mutually agreed upon social activity in public, together, as a couple.

So now you are equipped with these personal defense weapons on your holster, you now know the definition of a game, and the definition of dating. Just that knowledge itself put you in front of 50% of men who don't have a clue. Those 2 definitions combined are called the "dating Game" and we are here to make you a game changer.

Chapter 9

A Breath of Fresh Ass

Ok so women, let's talk about the average looking, average shape, mediocre woman from the age of 18-26, if she isn't already married, have been married before, or have children, or several sugar daddies then that's rare. As mentioned before about how women are raised and what the

believe, for the most part women aren't taught to be providers the financial providers for the family, nor is work a necessity, it's more of an abstract idea she may or may not choose to deal with, and more times than not if she does choose to work higher paying jobs, its subconsciously so she can meet a man making more than her so that she can live a wonderful like bearing children and siting around looking crazy. But within this time frame, how many dates do you think this woman has gone on? How many boyfriends, pseudo boyfriends, boy toys, sugar daddies, summer flings, and spring break flings she's had? In any given week how many times do you think she gets approached by men in public? On Facebook, on twitter? And we are just talking about a moderate average looking mediocre woman, not to fast, but not that slow either.

To answer your question, it is a better chance that she has not only been approached more often than you by the opposite sex, but that she's been in a considerable amount of situations where if she wanted sex it was easily obtained, and throughout those years, you would be fool to think that she hasn't had or still have several boyfriends, boy toys, sugar daddies, etc. not even counting the enormous numbers of ex boyfriends and creeper obsessed dates that still call and text her on the regular. So you see just an average woman at any given time even older, has men that if she wanted money or sex, are well within reach, so what comes with that? Skill, knowledge, training, she's got lots of training, once a woman reaches a certain point she already knows how to manipulate men, whether it's her on husband, boyfriend of desperate men she has wrapped around her finger. You do not want to be one of those men. This is game and you came equipped, with knowledge of the rules, how it's played, etc. you would think everyman would know this information as common sense, because it is common sense. Now that you now the rules, and basics on how it's played this should help form your strategies and techniques in approaching women.

The staple of all techniques is this: Let a woman know what your intentions are as soon as acceptably possibly in a respectful way.

That's it, really simple, hey what's your phone number? What's your name? where's your boyfriend?

GAME CHANGER: A Pimp's Memoires

I think your beautiful, I want you to be my girlfriend

Now when getting sex from women, more times than not it's a good idea to make her think you want her to be your girlfriend, or at the very least that you'll be around for more than just sex. Just like she manipulates and play games with men you can also do the same. And remember nowhere in the definition of dating did it say you only have to date one woman at a time. You don't have to play the same with only one person, you can play chess or checkers with any willing participant.

So the training is also a confidence booster, so you are training and gaining confidence at the same time, and how will you do this, simple. Say "HI" to at least one woman any woman, in public each day, or just send a message to one woman each day you don't know on social media. But the training and confidence booster can really be only practiced in real life situations, because the better your field real life game is, your social media game will increase exponentially, it's not the other way around, if you want to get good at basketball you have to physically get up and practice, not play basketball game on Xbox or PlayStation. Same concept

So once you begin to step out of your cocoon and begin to talk to women everyday by just saying HI that will gradually get you use to talking to women, it will also acclimate you you to how some woman will happily respond, some will look at you crazy, and some will say nothing

at all. And this is where you learn how to deal with rejection, because let's face it most of you guys are just scared to be rejected. This one application will boost your confidence, and teach you that in essence you only need one nice looking girl to smile at you and say hi, to offset the other 3 who didn't respond or looked at you weird. Once you start doing this, up your game and say hi to 2 women a day, 3 women a day, if you have time and aren't doing anything, instead of watching TV go to the mall, or your grocery store, with the intent of buying a dollar juice and to say hi to 2 different women. Once you actually start doing this, your confidence level will rise quickly, that is if you are rolling with the punches, before you know it you'll be so comfortable with talking to women that you'll start to just naturally come up with conversations.

This is purely a numbers game, 1 out of 10 women is a success, if you can get 3 oout of 10 women you meet to fuck you, that's pimp level game. Ok so some guys feel like 1 out of 10 is a low number, but if your saying hi or talking to 2 women a day for one week that 14 women, which means you have very good chances of actually land 1-2 dates per week bro! and that's just live field game, if you can manage to supplement that with POF or other free dating sites, you should be able to garner 2-4 women securing dates per week. That's allotting half an hour per day to social media and field game which is a total of 3.5 hours a week to get dates, that's a great investment.

The game is simple here's my basic line I say to any woman I DO NOT KNOW, in any particular setting it doesn't really matter, but I do look out for subtle signs, like what kind of mood is she in, typically if she's in a good mood, and she is laughing or giggly that a good sign, but that could just be her being friendly not actually flirting. Either way. Also it depends if she my waitress, or in a grocery store, and outdoor concert, etc. I encourage you to use this direct approach to a woman in passing, meaning if its possible you'll never see her again, I would never use this strategy on a girl I work with or go to school with, or see often

Hello

Wow you are beautiful, I really like how your necklace looks, it really brings out your eyes, and your complexion

Where's your boyfriend?

If she says she has one, I say "he must be the luckiest man alive" depending on her response if she opens to allow me to give her my number I will give her my number and keep it moving to the next woman

If she replies "I don't know where he is" or "I don't have one" then I simply ask

What's your phone number?

Guys with this approach its very simple it very easy and it takes less than 3 minutes, you are clearly stating you like her, by complimenting her, also that helps in buttering her up and feeling comfortable with you, you are asking if she's in a loyal relationship, do not ask her if she has a boyfriend, just ask her where is your boyfriend, that comes across way less invasive, and forces her to think where is sorry cheating ass it at, which I've scored numbers that way as well as the girl gets angry at the fact she doesn't know where he is, and you're in front of her being nice and flirtatious so why not give you her number

Getting a girl's phone number is very easy, and that just allows you to call and text, this is also where you introduce yourself if she is in fact giving you the phone number, hi my name is Tim and btw what's your name? I get phone numbers before I even get the girls name, heck sometimes I forget to get the name as long as I have that number. That's the quick easy proven way to get a date and get laid.

Now I typically like to allow some time to elapse before I consider calling or texting her, because if she had a very good first impression of you or felt that there was chemistry she going to tell her friends and she will think about you, and wonder when you will call. If she was just being nice then she won't think too much about it, either way, you gave her an ego boost. I use to wait 5 days before I texted or called and actually that worked great, but I think that's a bit long, but I will say wait at least 24 hours, at the very minimum, at least 24 hours but less than 3 days, is the good window to text or call her. And from there just be yourself,

Chapter 10

A Recap

So now we must talk about how to approach women we work with, go to school with, church with, etc. basically you use the same strategy but instead of over three minutes you can do it over a longer span of time, because mainly you will be able to get to know this woman, and see if you even like her your dam self, whereas the other approach is for a woman you may never physically see again in your life unless you 2 plan to sit and meet. In a setting where you see this woman, make sure you talk to her about mundane things, and get a feel for her, in general a woman will bring up her husband or boyfriend within a relatively short period of time subconsciously if she isn't into you any way, but if you build rapport with her and she never mentions her man, then go for it.

So in review u can use this same very simple technique to approach woman. Remember there are 2 different categories. 1 women you know. 2women you don't know. First thing is the confidence booster which is saying Hi to at least one real woman in person per day, the second week increase that to 2 women per day if possible, even if you have to drivel to the market or take a bus downtown. So the slate is simple.

Hello how are you doing?

Compliment here

Ask where's your boyfriend

Ask for her number, and exchange names

GAME CHANGER: A Pimp's Memoires

This is just a very plain jane basic approach that tends to cater to men's confidence, keeps the interaction fairly short, build up contacts in your phone, and is a template that once master you can tweak it and change it and improve upon it once you are at the stage where speaking to women comes second nature to you

Once you have the number wait 1-3 days to either call or text her, and from that point the best advice is being yourself. My job is to build your confidence, teach you proven simple strategies that work to get numbers, and set you up for as many potential dates as possible, what you choose to do from there on out is completely your decision the skies the limit.

With some of the backdrop information provided above, you are armed with the basic essentials to be able to be a force in the dating game, remember these keys

Never start out trying to be friends

Make your intentions known early on (because if she's not interested you can move on to the next one, we don't spend weeks and months chasing women who just want boy toys)

You are a confident handsome professional ladies' man who keeps cool and doesn't get nervous.

So we can begin to talk about some other factors that are important to dating, because some of us live in big urban cities, and some of us live in the rural areas the actual potential to even find women to practice on differs, but either way try your best to practice on as many women as possible.

Hygiene. It is important whatever your style is, that you are clean, if you have a beard or lots of hair make sure its groomed, try and wear clothes that are trendy but simple. A polo collared shirt with a nice pair of jeans is perfectly fine, whatever you choose to wear or whatever style you have just be clean and well groomed, fresh breath, clean undies and socks etc., all the things you learned when you were a child still applies

Your physical appearance, although with my techniques and teachings, which will enable any man of any size of any type of job or career to get laid, it is still important that you do realize being healthy is important, because ultimately women want men they can make healthy babies with. I don't expect you to be chiseled overnight, but start watching how you eat if you are a heavier man, and do pushups and sit ups every day, and walk for at least 20 minutes a day stay away from sodas, and juices, use coffee in moderation, and try to avoid carbs, or white foods such as "rice, bread, pasta, potatoes" and try to limit your intake of sugar, just following that simple diet and sticking to lean meats and vegetables, you'll begin to lose weight, anywhere between 1-3 lbs. per week that anywhere between 4-12lbs in a month!

If you are a man on the very slim side of the spectrum, again do push up and sit ups every day, walk /run 20 minutes a day, and supplement your diet with very high protein shakes, you can but tasty relatively cheap protein powders at Walmart this will allow you to gain some mass, even if it's just 1-2 pounds per week that 4-10 lbs. per month!

Everyone looks good in black, all women know this because they all have that black dress and black legging tights or the yoga pants they all love to wear, because let's be honest those tight yoga pants makes us men go crazy and almost makes any woman of any shape look better, same for men, black polo shirts and black t shirts with jeans or black gym shorts even whether big tall skinny or short takes out some of the things we don't like about our bodies. Haircuts are a must, and groom your facial hair.

Smelling good isn't as important as you may think, being clean is. we all have pheromones and this is what ultimately is important. According to Wikipedia. A pheromone is a secreted or excreted chemical factor that triggers a social response in members of the same species. Pheromones are chemicals capable of acting outside the body of the secreting individual to impact the behavior of the receiving individual. There are alarm pheromones, sex pheromones, and many others that affect behavior or physiology.

Basically everyone emits pheromones through sweat hence body odor, everyone has it, the best strategy is to pick a body spray or cologne that you like, and apply it lightly so that it doesn't over power your pheromones, that's why sometimes woman can be more aggressive toward men after an intense workout when they have sweated and released more pheromones profusely, I encourage you to do more research on this matter as it can be very scientific

LOVE

[4] Love is patient, love is kind. It does not envy, it does not boast, it is not proud. [5] It does not dishonor others, it is not self-seeking, it is not easily angered, it keeps no record of wrongs. [6] Love does not delight in evil but rejoices with the truth. [7] It always protects, always trusts, always hopes, always perseveres.

[8] Love never fails. But where there are prophecies, they will cease; where there are tongues, they will be stilled; where there is knowledge, it will pass away.

1 Corinthians 13:4-8 New International Version (NIV)

If I have the gift of prophecy and can fathom all mysteries and all knowledge, and if I have a faith that can move mountains, but have not love, I am nothing.

1 Corinthians 13:2 New International Version (NIV)

If I give all I possess to the poor and surrender my body to the flames, but have not love, I gain nothing.

1 Corinthians 13:3 New International Version (NIV)

Love is a highly misunderstood concept although the word itself is thrown around in almost every syntax imaginable. In its highest form Love is unconditional and accepting of all things. That is to include both good and evil. Love is not an embracing of something but merely an acceptance of what it is (whether that is firmly understood or not) and letting it blossom of its own accord. Love is also patient and kind, keeping no record of wrongs. In light of that information ninety percent of relationships claiming to be based on Love are found to be anything but:

'Selfishness is of degree; it is not absolute. And who is there who is not selfish to a degree? The body-mind cannot think of anything that is not of the senses. A man's body-mind will tell him that at death he and his family will cease to be; that he should get and enjoy all that he can get out of life; that he should not bother about the future or the people of the future; that it will not matter what happens to the people of the future- they will all die.'

-"Democracy is Self-Government", Howard Waldwin Percival

Death, in a sense, is a sort of super power. For, we see in a most honest perception, that those enabled with super human abilities will inevitably do for themselves. Absolute power corrupts absolutely. Usually when we think of death we think of it in terms of a debilitating capacity. How can this be when death makes human beings align more so with the selfish and inane? Although it is not death but the fear of death that makes people self-centered, self-serving and low. Instead of letting go of temporal things they flounder to grasp what is not real and will not last. For what? The logic is not sound. If we are to perish after some interval of time would it not make more sense to help one another, to cultivate something lasting and live not for one's self but for others? Perhaps, perhaps not. It seems as though humanity is not taking the fact of the mutable and temporary to heart but is, instead, musing in the illusion that it will live temporally in the physical. Though, in my belief, the inner portion of a person is unbounded by time and space and will live forever, that does not mean we get to act like asses while 'alive'. To me death, once met through courage and acceptance, is not only humbling but liberating. Without the phase-jump of death we would remain, inevitably, dull. Life and Death are intimately tied in to Love. For we exist in Love operating under precious laws of balance. Upon death our selfishness is toned down to serious degrees, for what we so sorely cling to is ripped from us and we imminently transmute into a new state- whatever that may be.

In the musings on creation it is rarely taken into account that both good and evil exists and so it must stand that, whether they were integrally designed or not, that they are there. In fighting against one or the other we come to much egregious error and suffering. Moreso, there is a current mode of thinking called "The Secret" in which it is said that one's thoughts are ultimately brought forth onto the living plane from simply holding intention. If this were True everyone would have what they wanted. However, the creation is not an ego based dynamic. EVERYTHING, from smallest to largest, from comprehendible to unknown, is taken into account. Even further, it is plain to see that the Universe itself prefers balance over favor which is consequentially expressed in paradigms like the law of conservation of mass and energy. Even the forces that bind us and give us motion are so steadily and precisely operating on principles similar to modes of mathematical equality that they are never found to be anything but balanced. I made that argument to support my own notion that creation is based on this dynamic of Love. After entering into creation each being is given free will to act in accordance with or against natural law. The Universal system itself always maintains its integrity but a man need not follow its ways. However, there are always repercussions for going against what is established in supreme intelligence and balance. Those consequences are namely death be it spiritual or physical. A man may ignore gravity and he is allowed to do just that but its force will still operate on him in conjunction with his standing condition regarding physical law. A man may claim to do good works but his actions are always in contrast to those laws which we may never understand in physical form (giving rise to notions of karma or judgment). Emanuel Swedenborg expounds upon this concept in his own channeled writings:

'There are in man from the Lord two capacities whereby he is distinguished from beasts. One of these is the ability to understand what is true and what is good; this is called rationality,
and is a capacity of his understanding. The other is an ability to do what is true and good; this is called freedom, and is a capacity of his will. For man by virtue of his rationality is able to think
whatever he pleases, either with or against God, either with or against the neighbor; he is also able to will and to do what he thinks; but when he sees evil and fears punishment, he is able, by virtue of his freedom, to abstain from doing it.'

-Angelic Wisdom Concerning Divine Love and Wisdom

The True application of this concept comes from the freedom it brings. My primary example will be that concerning the Garden of Eden. Before Adam and Even partook of the fruit of knowledge of good and evil they were innocent and happy without a care in the world. After ingesting the notion they were suddenly ashamed and bold enough to lie to God as God searched for them. All notions and philosophies of the meaning or reality of the story aside, its base concept predicates and invaluable lesson. Namely that the knowledge of good and evil leads to death of the spirit and rebellion against what is already supreme and established. Prior to eating the fruit Adam and Eve were in Love. They accepted their condition, where they were and what was happening without question. In that innocence they were alive, happy and enjoying creation. Once they fell to the base of duality they could no longer enjoy that supreme unity. Many would say that that last state is evil. Quite the contrary, it is what it is. The only thing keeping humanity from ultimately being at peace and re-entering innocence is the consistent need to judge things as right or wrong. Without fear or prejudice about life or death or the contents therein rests a holy liberation. That liberation comes from a steady de-conditioning of western thought and a raising of the mind into an age-old principle of Love whose reality is far beyond definition and succinctly more holy. Emanuel Swedenborg outlines this topic in several works but makes the most sincere connection between humanity and genesis in his works, "Aracana Coelestia":

'But of the tree of the knowledge [scientia] of good and evil, thou shalt not eat of it; for in the day that thou eatest thereof, thou shalt die.
These words, taken together with those just explained, signify that it is allowable to become acquainted with what is true and good by means of every perception derived from the Lord, but not from self and the world; that is, we are not to inquire into the mysteries of faith by means of the things of sense and of the memory [per sensualia et scientifica], for in this case the celestial of faith is destroyed.
127. A desire to investigate the mysteries of faith by means of the things of sense and of the memory was not only the cause of the fall of the posterity of the most ancient church, as treated

of in the following chapter, but it is also the cause of the fall of every church; for hence come not only falsities, but also evils of life... The worldly and corporeal man says in his heart, If I am not instructed concerning the faith, and everything relating to it, by means of the things of sense, so that I may see, or by means of those of the memory *[scientifica],* so that I may understand, I will not believe; and he confirms himself in this by the consideration that natural things cannot be contrary to spiritual. Thus he is desirous of being instructed from things of sense in what is celestial and Divine, which is as impossible as it is for a camel to go through the eye of a needle; for the more he desires to grow wise by such means, the more he blinds himself, till at length he believes nothing, not even that there is anything spiritual, or that there is eternal life. This comes from the principle which he assumes. And this is to "eat of the tree of the knowledge of good and evil," of which the more anyone eats, the more dead he becomes.'

-Page 77 Arcana Coelestia Volume I

'And out of the ground made Jehovah God to grow every tree desirable to behold, and good for food; the tree of lives also, in the midst of the garden, and the tree of the knowledge [scientiae] *of good and evil.* A "tree" signifies perception; a "tree desirable to behold," the perception of truth; a "tree good for food," the perception of good; the "tree of lives," love and the faith thence derived; the "tree of the knowledge of good and evil," faith derived from what is sensuous, that is, from mere memory-knowledge.'

-Page 67 Arcana Coelestia Volume I

'Because from the love of self, that is, their own love, they began to believe nothing that they did not apprehend by the senses, the sensuous part is represented by the "serpent"; the love of self, or their own love, by the "woman"; and the rational by the "man."'

-Page 100 Arcana Coelestia Volume I

'In ancient times those were called "serpents" who had more confidence in sensuous things than in revealed ones. But it is still worse at the present day, for now there are persons who not only disbelieve everything they cannot see and feel, but who also confirm themselves in such incredulity by knowledges *[scientifica]* unknown to the ancients, and thus occasion in themselves a far greater degree of blindness.'

-Page 103 Arcana Coelestia Volume I

Humanity struggles with the application of its thought into action because of the consistent filtering process going through what is deemed good or evil. In using the singular definition of Love as Unconditional acceptance and its goods presented in Corinthians we can obliterate mass confusion.

'The unbearable nature of evil; the fact that it is scandalous, and if there does not exist a reason and an energy capable of overcoming it, the spontaneous temptation is to expunge it from oneself, from one's group... to project it outside, so as to get it in front of you and in some way to contain and master it. It is a problem of insufferance: we are not able to bear the suffering that evil brings about so we create a mechanism of resentment against it that takes concrete form—so to speak—against someone. It is a deep, insidious resentment that can even take the form of humanitarianism. Just think of certain ways of looking at pathetic cases in order to justify divorce, abortion, genetic manipulation, euthanasia.... In reality, it is to alleviate our own anguish and satisfy our own resentment toward a suffering that makes us feel our powerlessness.
So what does it mean to say that in this game "freedom stops in front of the experience of limitation"?
It is the basic question. Freedom is autonomous adherence to the good. But in its very capacity to adhere, it is put to the test,

because adherence to the good passes through choice, which is a power exposed to risk and drama. The dualist vision is petrified by the experience of evil and cannot manage to look at itself as the locus where the drama is played out. But by doing this, it does not succeed in living the depth of freedom. Throwing evil out, equating it with something "other," means giving up the depth of one's own freedom.'

-Powerless Freedom: About Good and Evil [http://www.traces-cl.com/june03/powerless.html]

In the Qabalistic teachings the tree of knowledge of good and evil is known as Daath or 'the void'. It is described as the doorway leading in to or out of Eden depending on how that knowledge is used. Here is an example:

'That is why Daath is called the Tree of Knowledge of Good and Evil, because there are two potential outcomes of using this door.
Here we have to clarify that the words good and evil in the context of Daath are not as simple as the dualistic notion of right and wrong, or good and evil, in the way we always think of it. It is not limited to that sense of duality. It is much richer and deeper than simply "good" and "bad," like the way a child thinks of good or bad, or the way we think of our morals or ethics as good or bad, or the good and bad guys in the movies. That form of thinking is very limited. It is dualistic, it is intellectual. It does not encompass how nature actually works. Nature in itself is not good or bad, it just "is." Nature functions according to laws, and Daath is the same. Daath expresses certain laws, and by application of the knowledge (Daath), we arrive at certain consequences, or results.'

-

http://74.125.113.132/search?q=cache:UtZmi00niNIJ:gnosticte
achings.org/the-teachings-of-gnosis/lectures-by-gnostic-

instructors/daath-the-doorway-to-knowledge-
1+judgment+daath&hl=en&strip=1

This last quote expresses what I mean in very simple terms:

"If you've got Love in your heart, whatever you do from that
moment out is likely to be right. If you've got that one True note
ringing inside of you, then whatever you do is going to be ok.
It's Love, always Love."

-Ken Kesey

Let me not to the marriage of true minds
Admit impediments. Love is not love
Which alters when it alteration finds,
Or bends with the remover to remove:
Oh, no! it is an ever-fixed mark,
That looks on tempests and is never shaken,
It is the star to every wandering bark,
Whose worth's unknown, although his height be taken.
Love's not Time's fool, though rosy lips and cheeks
Within his bending sickle's compass come;
Love alters not with his brief hours and weeks,
But bears it out even to the edge of doom.
If this be error and upon me proved,
I never writ, nor no man ever loved.

-Shakespeare Sonnet 116

Final Chapter

Evolution

If you read all of this, I promise you are now much different than before. If you read all of this and are practicing it then you are not only different than before but you are getting laid and evolved. This information will change you and as you continue to evolve you will have to make a decision: "what now". Pussy doesn't rule you- you rule it. After a while it was no longer the fear of rejection but the fear of acceptance that haunted me as I looked at a pretty girl. I would think "fuck- What if she says yes- Then I'll have to deal with her- if I fuck her that's time and energy". It really liberates you when you are no longer a slave to something that easily attainable. Groveling over women is like going outside and lusting for dirt. You can get dirt anywhere. Even social media teaches us to gawk and behold this pretty girl and that beautiful woman, but did you ever stop to think: why? You have to realize that attraction and romance are just another realm of power struggle between humans: "all is fair in Love and War". So now you are no longer being trampled by worthless scum but are the King of your very own Domain. Fill it with your worthwhile citizens and bring prosperity to your world.

I'll tell you one of the things I did after I learned all of this. I started to pick up women and do experiments regarding love. I studied about the different forms of love (eros, agape and philia) for a couple years, as well as various forms of tantra and bdsm. I put it all together creating "programs" for relationships in which I would subject women to various affections that made them fall deeply in love. Then I would see what could be done to intensify and erect the foundations of that love further. The one problem I ran into was POSSESSIVENESS. We talked about relationships and these are actually a true hindrance to human evolution at large. Mating pairs is good, that enhances us and gives us chemical, psychological pleasure as well as new experience to build our imaginative domains. But when we are locked up with another person we atrophy. Unfortunately the primary objective of most women is to lock up a man with value. Don't let that happen. If you do you lose your ability to create and grow. Don't forget- women is the inhibitive force and man is the creative force. She will place restrictive forms on your finances, your time, your life and your creativity. If you want to remain a true Alpha Male you will need to stay single until the time comes when you are ready to be placed in that restriction. It is not a bad thing. All the Universe is built of force (creativity) and (form) but now that you are aware of that fact you have choices to make on when and where you want those forces to act in your romantic life. You are now stepping into the realm of energetic manipulation. Use that ability for good or evil it is entirely up to you. With this information a much better world can be built as the true Men step up, take control and guide relationships on the right path. It might seem like I spent a lot of time just fucking bitches and I did. However, I also spent a lot of time telling them beautiful stories and relaying information to them about all the divine things I learned in quantum physics, psychology and spiritual teachings regarding the architecture of reality. Once I told a girl a personal story of mine, a fictional story in my head I've worked on for years, and she cried. You can captivate these women but don't forget, my friend, that you now have the opportunity to lead, enhance and evolve these women.

References

-Elite

http://elitedaily.com/dating/gentlemen/women-chase/

-Rochester

http://www.pas.rochester.edu/~stte/phy104-F00/notes-2.html

-theproblemismen

http://www.theproblemismen.com/rants/badboys#ixzz48zK
6CS20

-majorleaguedating

http://www.majorleaguedating.com/traits-bad-boys-nice-guys/

Printed in Great Britain
by Amazon